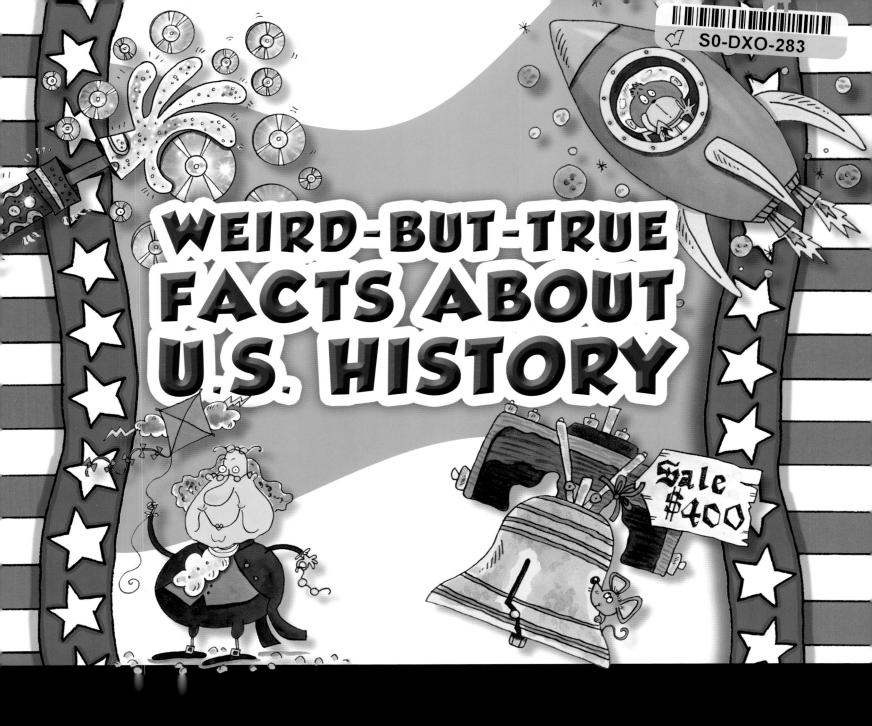

WEIRD-BUT-TRUE FACTS ABOUT U.S. HISTORY

Sale $400

RiverStream Illustrated
Great Reading • Real Learning

Published by RiverStream Publishing
PO Box 364
Mankato, MN 56002
www.riverstreampublishing.com

RiverStream Publishing reprinted with permission of
The Child's World®.

ISBN 9781614734215
LCCN 2012946528

Printed in the United States of America
Mankato, MN

1 2 3 4 5 CG 16 15 14 13
RiverStream Publishing—Corporate Graphics,
Mankato, MN—022014—1051CGW14

About the Author

Arnold Ringstad lives in Minneapolis, Minnesota. He wishes there were underground moving sidewalks there.

About the Illustrator

A former greeting card artist, Mernie Gallagher-Cole is a freelance illustrator with over 28 years experience illustrating for children. Her charming illustrations can be found on greeting cards, party goods, games, puzzles, children's books, and now e-books and educational game apps! She lives in Philadelphia with her husband and two children.

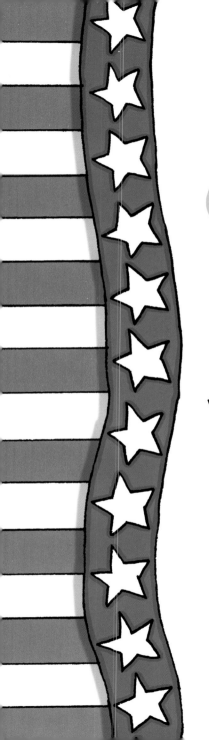

TABLE OF CONTENTS

INTRODUCTION

U.S. history is filled with famous firsts, odd government activities, and bizarre plans. The United States has been around for less than 250 years, but it has already seen many weird events. From the Emperor of the United States to abandoned plans for a dome over New York City, get ready to learn about these unusual parts of U.S. history. And don't forget, these facts are all true!

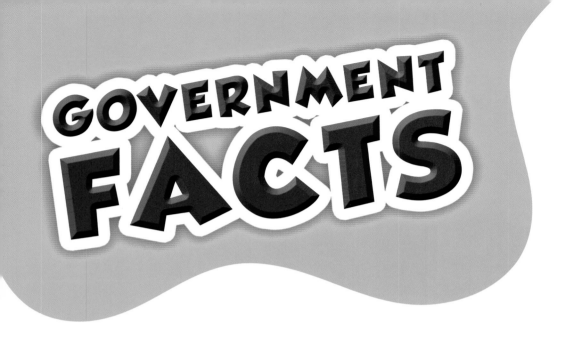

GOVERNMENT FACTS

Members of Congress can send official mail for free.

This is known as a "franking privilege."

Only one U.S. congressperson voted against U.S. involvement in both World War I and World War II.

Her name was Jeanette Rankin. She was also the first congresswoman in U.S. history.

James Byrnes served as a U.S. representative, a U.S. senator, a Supreme Court justice, and the governor of South Carolina.

He never attended high school or college.

In 1959, the U.S. vice president and the Soviet premier had a debate in a kitchen.

Richard Nixon and Nikita Khrushchev were in a model kitchen at a home exhibition in Moscow, Russia, when they had the famous debate.

The longest serving senator was in office for more than 51 years.

West Virginia senator Robert C. Byrd held his seat from January 3, 1959, until June 28, 2010. That's 51 years, five months, and 26 days!

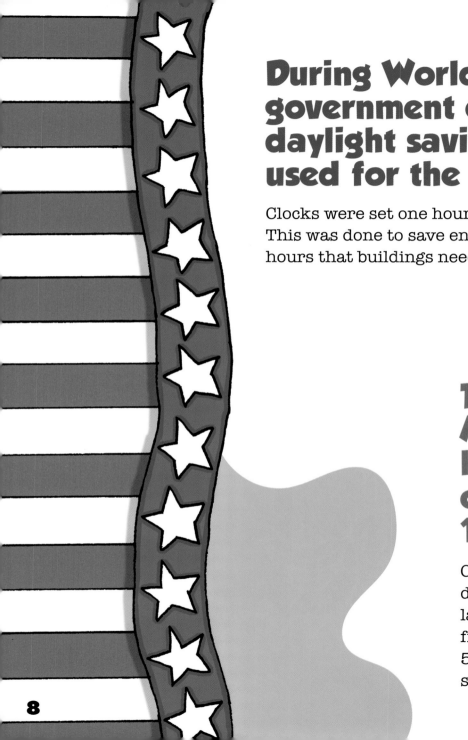

During World War II, the government ordered that daylight saving time be used for the entire year.

Clocks were set one hour ahead of standard time. This was done to save energy by having fewer hours that buildings needed to use lights.

The Washington Monument stood less than one-third completed between 1854 and 1877.

Construction began in 1848 but was delayed due to the U.S. Civil War and a lack of money. When construction finally finished in 1884, it reached slightly over 555 feet (169 m) tall. It is still the tallest stone structure in the world.

A U.S. representative beat a senator with a cane in 1856.

They strongly disagreed about the issue of slavery. Preston Brooks hit Charles Sumner with a cane until he was unconscious.

The ironwork in the dome of the U.S. Capitol building weighs almost 9 million pounds (4 million kg).

This is about as much as 600 elephants. The iron dome was finished in 1866.

FAMOUS AMERICANS

In 1970, the singer Elvis Presley visited President Nixon in the White House.

Elvis gave the president gifts, including family photos and a pistol.

Benjamin Franklin invented bifocals because he was tired of carrying two pairs of glasses— one for up close viewing and one to see far away.

Neil Armstrong, the first man to walk on the moon, had experience flying more than 200 types of airplanes.

He also flew two kinds of spacecraft, Gemini 8 and Apollo 11.

In 2004, computer tycoon Bill Gates received 4 million e-mails per day.

The singer Michael Jackson sold more than 750 million records while he was alive.

This is the most of any solo artist.

John Glenn, the first American to orbit Earth, later became the oldest person to ever fly in space.

He flew on the Space Shuttle Discovery in 1998 at the age of 77.

Baseball player Babe Ruth put leaves of lettuce under his hat to keep cool during games.

The author Mark Twain's real name was Samuel Langhorne Clemens.

Other pen names he used were Thomas Jefferson Snodgrass and Josh.

WEIRD IDEAS AND PLANS

In 1911, a member of the U.S. House of Representatives tried to pass a law to **abolish** the U.S. Senate.

The city of Philadelphia almost got rid of the **Liberty Bell**.

In 1828, the Pennsylvania city rebuilt the tower on top of the State House building. They paid a bell maker $400 for a new bell, and he was supposed to take away the old bell. However, he argued that the bell was more expensive to haul away than it was worth, so he left it. Later, his heirs argued that they owned the bell. Finally, they agreed to loan it to the city permanently.

In 1958, there were plans to explode a nuclear weapon on the moon.

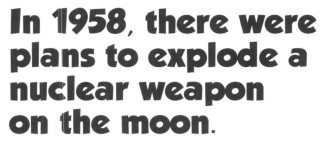

The U.S. government wanted to show off its technological achievements to the world. Instead, they decided to simply land on the moon.

A statue of a shirtless, muscular George Washington was made in 1840 as a tribute to the president.

It was intended to be placed in the U.S. Capitol building. When it was unveiled, people found it funny or offensive. It was moved outside to the lawn of the Capitol a few years later. It is now on the second floor of the National Museum of American History in Washington, DC.

In 1959, the U.S. Postal Service experimented with sending mail by **missile**.

A cruise missile that normally carried a nuclear **warhead** had its bomb replaced by containers of mail. The test worked, but it was too expensive to continue doing.

In 1956, the architect Frank Lloyd Wright designed a mile-high skyscraper called "The Mile High Illinois."

It would have been more than four times taller than the Empire State Building in New York City. It was part of his dream city plan, Broadacre City.

In 1960, the engineer Buckminster Fuller planned a 2-mile (3.2-km) dome to be built over part of Manhattan in New York City.

It was supposed to reduce air pollution and allow people to control the weather.

In the early 1900s, there was a plan to install underground moving sidewalks in New York City to replace subways.

AMERICAN FIRSTS

The first American copper pennies were ordered on May 8, 1792.

George Washington signed an act that allowed for the purchase of up to 150 tons (136 metric tons) of copper to make the coins.

The first American book in English was written in 1608.

Written by Captain John Smith, it was a description of the history of the Virginia colony up to that point.

The
History of
the
Virgina Colony
1608
by
Capt. John Smith

#1

Albert II was the first American monkey to fly in space.

In 1949, he reached an altitude of more than 80 miles (130 km) in a rocket.

Theodore Roosevelt was the first American to win a Nobel Peace Prize.

He won it in 1906 for helping end a war between Russia and Japan.

American and Soviet spacecraft met for the first time in 1975.

The two shuttles locked together in space. The crewmembers shook hands, exchanged gifts, and conducted science experiments.

The first American town to name itself after George Washington did so in 1776.

This was only one year into the Revolutionary War and 13 years before he became president.

Harvard University, established in 1636, was the first American university.

The oldest building still standing as of 2012 was built in 1720.

The first American electronic computer was made in 1946.

It was called ENIAC, meaning Electronic Numerical Integrator And Computer. It weighed more than 30 tons (27 metric tons).

OTHER AMAZING HISTORY FACTS

During President Richard Nixon's impeachment trial, he was accused of illegally raising the price of McDonald's hamburgers.

Some of the first English settlers in the United States mysteriously disappeared.

In 1587, 115 colonists were left at the Roanoke colony while their ship returned to England to get supplies. When the ship came back three years later, the settlers had vanished. The only clue to their fate was the word "Croatoan" carved into a wooden post.

There is only one royal palace in the United States.

It is located in Hawaii and was used by the Hawaiian king and queen until they were overthrown in 1893. Today it is a museum.

During the American Revolution, some brides wore red dresses instead of white ones.

They did this to show their support for the war.

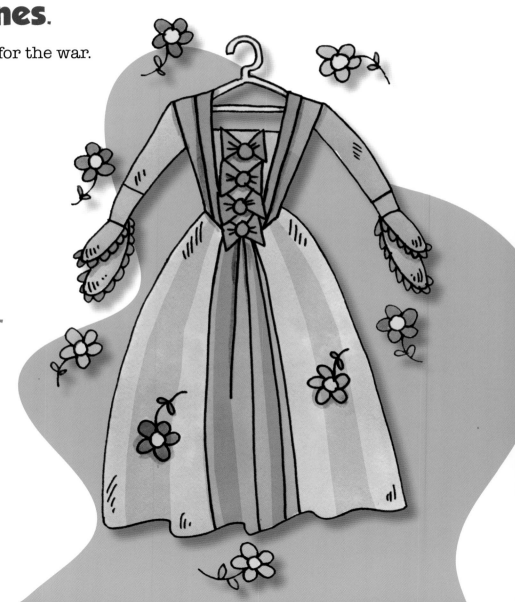

The addition of Alaska increased the size of the United States by almost 20 percent.

It was purchased from Russia for $7.2 million in 1867.

In 1986, people held hands across the United States.

The event was called Hands Across America. More than 5 million people participated, forming a line that stretched over 4,000 miles (6,400 km).

In 1945, a woman survived falling more than 75 stories in an Empire State Building elevator.

A B-52 bomber accidentally hit the building, breaking the elevator cables. The elevator's shock absorbers made the landing soft enough to survive.

A New York dairy farmer showed his support for President Andrew Jackson in 1837 by creating a 1,400-pound (630 kg) wheel of cheese.

The cheese was 11 feet (3.4 m) around and 2 feet (0.6 m) thick.

There are more than 137 million items in the collection of the Smithsonian Institution.

They range from dinosaur bones to **prehistoric** tools to moon rocks. It is the largest museum collection in the world.

In 1849, there was a riot in New York City over one of British playwright William Shakespeare's plays.

Playgoers did not approve of the lead actor, and 22 people died.

In 1893, a U.S. representative proposed changing the name of the country to "the United States of the World."

The representative was Lucas Miller from Wisconsin.

The right arm and torch of the Statue of Liberty were on display at a fair in Philadelphia in 1876.

Visitors could pay 50 cents to climb inside. This raised the money to finish the rest of the statue.

In the 1800s, a man named Joshua Norton declared himself Emperor of the United States.

He lived in San Francisco, wore an elaborate uniform, and ordered the U.S. Congress to dissolve. Up to 10,000 people lined the streets to pay tribute when he died.

Statue of Liberty

Climb the Arm 50¢

In January 1919, 2 million gallons (7.6 million L) of hot molasses flowed through the streets of Boston, Massachusetts.

A 50-foot (15-m) tank exploded, releasing the molasses and killing 21 people.

Benjamin Franklin thought the turkey would be a better national bird than the bald eagle.

He said that the turkey is a "much more respectable bird."

GLOSSARY

abolish (uh-BALL-ish)
To abolish is to get rid of something. Someone proposed a law to abolish the U.S. Senate.

bifocals (BYE-fo-culls)
Bifocals are eyeglasses that have two different kinds of lenses built in to them. Benjamin Franklin needed bifocals to see well.

missile (MISS-uls)
A missile is a weapon that is shot at a target. A pilot can fire a missile at a target far away.

prehistoric (pree-hiss-TOR-ik)
Something prehistoric happened before the invention of writing. The museum has prehistoric tools on display.

riot (RYE-it)
A riot is a violent protest. There was a riot in the city.

skyscraper (SKY-scrape-ur)
A skyscraper is a very tall building. Frank Lloyd Wright wanted to build a skyscraper.

warhead (WAR-hed)
The warhead is the part of a bomb or missile that explodes. The missile carried a nuclear warhead.

LEARN MORE

BOOKS

The Editors of Klutz. *The Slightly Odd United States of America*. Palo Alto, CA: Klutz, 2010.

Lederer, Richard, and Caroline McCullagh. *American Trivia: What We All Should Know about U.S. History, Culture & Geography*. Layton, UT: Gibbs Smith, 2012.

WEB SITES

Visit our Web site for links about weird U.S. history facts: **childsworld.com/links**

Note to Parents, Teachers, and Librarians: We routinely verify our Web links to make sure they are safe and active sites. So encourage your readers to check them out!

Buckminster Fuller Dome

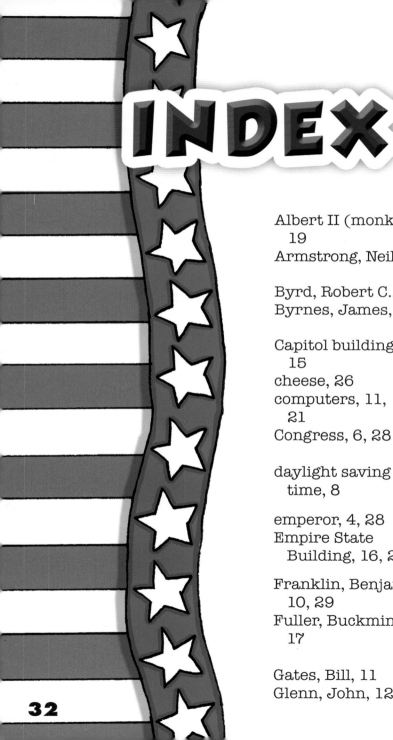

INDEX